GREAT ENTREPRENEURS
IN U.S. HISTORY

Andrew Carnegie
and the Steel Industry

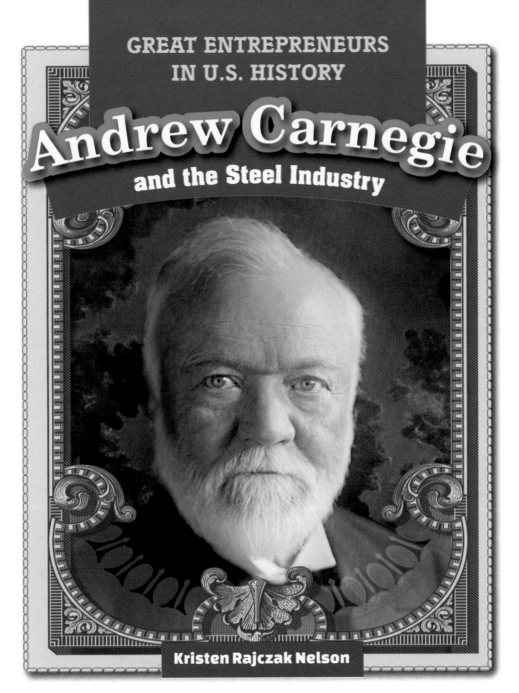

Kristen Rajczak Nelson

PowerKiDS
press.

New York

Published in 2017 by The Rosen Publishing Group, Inc.
29 East 21st Street, New York, NY 10010

First Edition

Editor: Sarah Machajewski
Book Design: Mickey Harmon

Photo Credits: Cover, pp. 1–4, 6–10, 12–20, 22–28, 30–32 (series design) Melodist/Shutterstock.com; cover (Andrew Carnegie), pp. 1, 23 Everett Historical/Shutterstock.com; p. 5 courtesy of Library of Congress; pp. 6, 8 ullstein bild/Contributor/Getty Images; p. 7 Robert Welch/Contributor/Hulton Archive/Getty Images; p. 9 https://upload.wikimedia.org/wikipedia/commons/5/51/Andrew_and_Thomas_Carnegie_-_Project_Gutenberg_eText_17976.jpg; p. 11 Interim Archives/Contributor/Getty Images; p. 13 Imagno/Contributor/Getty Images; p. 14 Hulton Archive/Stringer/Hulton Archive/Getty Images; p. 15 UniversalImagesGroup/Contributor/Universal Images Group/Getty Images; p. 16 https://upload.wikimedia.org/wikipedia/commons/0/01/Andrew_Carnegie_circa_1878_-_Project_Gutenberg_eText_17976.jpg; p. 17 https://upload.wikimedia.org/wikipedia/commons/5/5d/Steel_industry_inside_loc.jpg; p. 19 Oleksiy Mark/Shutterstock.com; p. 21 DW labs Incorporated/Shutterstock.com; p. 25 FPG/Staff/Getty Images; p. 27 Fotosearch/Stringer/Getty Images; p. 29 Buyenlarge/Contributor/Getty Images.

Cataloging-in-Publication Data

Names: Nelson, Kristen Rajczak.
Title: Andrew Carnegie and the steel industry / Kristen Rajczak Nelson.
Description: New York : PowerKids Press, 2017. | Series: Great entrepreneurs in U.S. history | Includes index.
Identifiers: ISBN 9781499421156 (pbk.) | ISBN 9781499421170 (library bound) | ISBN 9781499421163 (6 pack)
Subjects: LCSH: Carnegie, Andrew, 1835-1919–Juvenile literature. | Industrialists–United States–Biography-Juvenile literature. | Steel industry and trade–United States–History–Juvenile literature. | Philanthropists–United States–Biography–Juvenile literature.
Classification: LCC CT275.C3 N45 2017 | DDC 338.7′672′092–d23

Manufactured in the United States of America

CPSIA Compliance Information: Batch #BS16PK: For Further Information contact Rosen Publishing, New York, New York at 1-800-237-9932

Contents

A Historic Life

Andrew Carnegie's life is a great example of the American dream coming true. He worked in a factory as a young man but eventually worked his way up to own several companies. He was an **immigrant** and mostly self-educated, but he became one of the wealthiest men in the United States during his life.

The modern steel industry owes much to Carnegie. From his early investments to the start of the Carnegie Steel Company, Carnegie had an incredible ability to sense what the future would hold. He brought **technology** to the United States that would become the industry standard.

Carnegie's role in the formation of the U.S. steel industry is only part of his **legacy**. Carnegie believed **philanthropy** was his most important calling. Almost 100 years after his death, he continues to give.

An entrepreneur is someone who organizes and manages a business or a business idea. Entrepreneurs like Andrew Carnegie must be brave and creative thinkers, as starting a new business can have lots of challenges.

Industrial Beginnings

Carnegie was born on November 25, 1835, in Dunfermline, Scotland. Carnegie's father was a weaver and came from a family of weavers. Carnegie was expected to learn the family trade. However, when Carnegie was about 12, steam-powered looms came to Dunfermline. His father lost his business. Carnegie's father and grandfather joined movements that fought for workers' rights, but they weren't successful.

Faced with poverty, Carnegie's mother opened a grocery store and also started fixing shoes. The hard times brought about by change in the weaving industry made an impression on Carnegie. He later wrote: "It was burnt into my heart then that my father had to beg for work. And then and there came the resolve that I would cure that when I got to be a man."

Carnegie's birthplace

The Industrial Revolution

The Carnegie family lived through the spread of the Industrial Revolution that occurred in Great Britain from around 1760 to 1840. During this time, the invention of new machines changed many industries, including cloth making and farming. Factories became more common, as did power sources such as coal, steam, and electricity. Great leaps in communication, such as the introduction of the **telegraph** and radio, occurred during the Industrial Revolution, too. Early cars, steam-powered trains, and sewing machines were introduced during this time as well.

A weaver is a person who creates fabrics such as cloth and linen. Carnegie's father performed his trade on a handloom much like this one.

To the United States!

After a short time, Carnegie's mother convinced her husband it was time to leave Scotland. She wanted the family to go to the United States. She believed there would be more opportunities there. In 1848, Carnegie, his parents, and his younger brother, Thomas, sailed from Scotland to New York City. Carnegie was about 12.

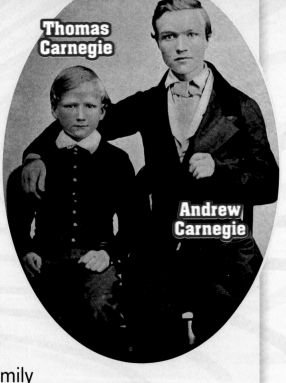

Thomas Carnegie

Andrew Carnegie

The Carnegies had to travel another three weeks to reach their new home in Allegheny, Pennsylvania, which is now part of Pittsburgh, Pennsylvania. Carnegie's mother had family there. At the time, Pittsburgh was the center of iron manufacturing in the United States. When the family settled, Carnegie's father took over a weaving shop and the family lived above it. However, the shop was unsuccessful and soon closed. Thousands of miles away from home, the Carnegies were once again facing poverty.

A Working Boy

Carnegie and his father both went to work in a cotton factory. Carnegie made $1.20 a week as a **bobbin** boy. That's $33.19 in today's money. When Carnegie was 14, he became a messenger in a telegraph office. Soon, he learned to use a telegraph, and, mostly by practicing by himself, became a telegraph operator. Carnegie's hard work impressed a man named Thomas Scott. In 1853, Scott made Carnegie his personal secretary and telegrapher at the Pennsylvania Railroad Company.

Carnegie made his first successful investment using advice he got from Scott. Later in life, Carnegie said, "I can see that first check of $10 **dividend** money. It was something new to all of us, for none of us had ever received anything but from toil." This means that until then, they worked for their money, instead of letting their money work for them.

Carnegie's father died when Carnegie was 16, making him the main supporter of the household. Any extra money he could make for his family went to good use.

Self-Schooled

Carnegie began working from the time his family arrived in the United States, so going to school every day wasn't an option. Instead, Carnegie found his own ways to learn. As a boy, he worked as a telegraph messenger, and he often delivered messages to a theater in Pittsburgh. Carnegie asked to make these deliveries at night so he could stay and watch the plays.

Carnegie was introduced to a kind of library when he was a boy working as a messenger. A gentleman named Colonel James Anderson allowed working boys to come to his library on Saturdays and borrow anything from his collection of about 400 books. Carnegie learned a great deal from reading the books Anderson made available and from his role as a **benefactor**.

Carnegie gave the money to build the Carnegie Library of Pittsburgh. It opened in 1895.

Letter to the Editor

In 1853, those who ran Anderson's library decided only certain boys could borrow books. They wanted to limit it to boys who worked for an employer to learn a trade without making money. That meant Carnegie couldn't use the library without paying a fee. So, he wrote letters to the editor of the *Pittsburgh Dispatch*. Carnegie argued that all working boys should be able to use the library, allowing the poor to have the opportunity to learn. The letters worked, and the library changed its rules!

War Interrupts

As Scott rose in the railroad company, so did Carnegie. He became the superintendent of the Pittsburgh division in 1859 at just 24. During the late 1850s, Carnegie also became a **shareholder** in the company that made the first railroad sleeper cars. This investment would make him a lot of money.

However, when the American Civil War broke out in 1861, business across the country stopped. Scott became the assistant secretary of war overseeing the railroads and telegraphs for the Union army. Carnegie traveled with him to Washington, D.C., and was put in charge of the government's telegraph operations. Carnegie even saw the war up close as the head of communications on the field at the First Battle of Bull Run.

The Story of the Sleeper Car

In his autobiography, Carnegie made it seem like he discovered the person who invented the sleeper car and then convinced Scott and others to invest in the idea. However, a Carnegie biographer later wrote that Carnegie hadn't played a big part in the deal at all! Scott and others from the Pennsylvania Railroad had already received shares of the inventor's company, some of which they put in Carnegie's name.

The story Carnegie told about the sleeper car gave the impression that he saw it as an invention of the future. People believed this because he made much of his later fortune by sensing future successes.

Iron and Industry

While working on the railroads during the Civil War, Carnegie saw how important iron was to their construction. He believed the iron industry would continue to grow after the war. Carnegie's brother had knowledge of ironworks, and Carnegie began to work with him to buy mills to produce iron. Around 1865, the brothers and a few other men started the Keystone Bridge Company.

By the mid-1860s, Carnegie was making about $50,000 a year. He was becoming an important industrial investor.

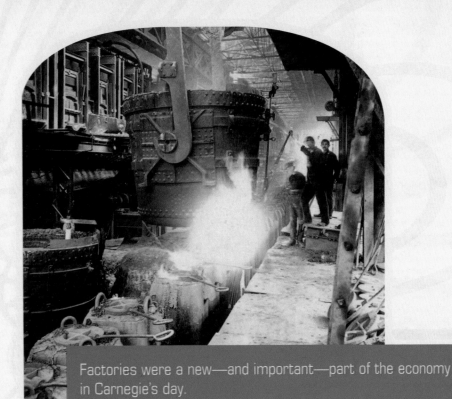
Factories were a new—and important—part of the economy in Carnegie's day.

They worked to replace wooden bridges with stronger ones made of iron. In 1865, the war ended and Carnegie left the Pennsylvania Railroad to work solely on his iron dreams.

In addition to Keystone, Carnegie and his brother bought a few mills and other holdings under the name Union Iron Mills. Carnegie also invested in an oil field in Pennsylvania that would eventually be worth $250,000!

Man of Steel

While visiting Great Britain in 1868, Carnegie learned about the Bessemer process, which is a way of making a large amount of iron into steel. He was sure steel, which is a strong and durable metal made from iron, was a material of the future.

Carnegie built the first steel plants in the United States made especially to produce steel using the Bessemer process. He was a full or part owner in the Homestead Steel Works; Carnegie, Phipps & Co.; and Carnegie Brothers & Co. By 1890, the United States was producing more steel than Great Britain, a change mostly credited to Carnegie.

By then, Carnegie was successfully using vertical integration. This means that he owned every step of the steelmaking process, from the coke fields and iron deposits to the railroads that sent the raw materials to his plants.

Homestead Strike

Despite Carnegie's past as a workingman fighting for opportunities, workers at the Homestead Steel Works plant still worked long hours for little money. They went on strike in 1892. The man in charge of the plant, Henry Frick, locked workers out and called in 300 men to try to stop the strike. The situation turned violent, and many people died. Carnegie was in Europe at the time, and he was accused of not doing more to fix the problem.

Carnegie was a smart businessman. He adopted new technology if it would make his product better or faster, such as the open-hearth furnace his plants began to use in the 1890s.

Making Money

In 1889, Carnegie combined all of his business holdings to form the Carnegie Steel Company. The following year, Carnegie Steel made $40 million. About $25 million went to Carnegie. The company continued to grow, even through a **depression** during the early 1890s. In 1890, construction of Carnegie Hall began in New York City.

Though one of the richest men in the United States, Carnegie hadn't been happy as a businessman for years. During the late 1860s, he wrote: "To continue much longer overwhelmed by business cares and with most of my thoughts wholly upon the way to make more money in the shortest time, must **degrade** me beyond hope of permanent recovery." Though he was good at making money, it wasn't his main goal.

Today, Carnegie Hall is one of the most respected concert halls in the United States.

The Gospel of Wealth

Carnegie's views of wealth were well known. In 1889, he wrote an article in the *North American Review* that became known as "The Gospel of Wealth." He stated his belief that rich people should use their money to take care of their families and to help other people.

Carnegie believed wealthy people should use their money to better the world around them. He seemed to see himself as a benefactor, much like Colonel James Anderson, who allowed Carnegie to use his library as a young man. However, Carnegie thought money, aid, and opportunity should only be for those who were willing to help themselves as well. *The Gospel of Wealth* is also the name of a book of essays written by Carnegie and published in 1900.

Carnegie wrote in "The Gospel of Wealth" that "the man who dies rich dies disgraced."

The Buyout

Carnegie's ability to see that iron and steel would be important industries of the future made him a lot of money. It also made the United States a leader in steel around the world. After spending so many years as a self-made businessman, Carnegie knew that competition made the American business world great. So when J. P. Morgan formed the United States Steel Corporation, Carnegie must have known competition would arise.

Yet, Carnegie wasn't interested in battling with Morgan. He was in his mid-60s and had a young daughter with his wife, Louise, whom he had married in the late 1880s. Instead, he sold Morgan the company for $480 million in 1901. After the deal was done, Morgan said, "Congratulations, Mr. Carnegie, you are now the richest man in the world."

Morgan was a very rich, powerful man in the early 1900s. He combined the Carnegie Steel Company with other steel companies to form U.S. Steel. It was the world's first billion-dollar company.

Giving It All Away

Without a company to run, Carnegie now had the freedom to do what he wanted to do—give back. Some of his first projects occurred even before he sold Carnegie Steel, such as giving money to build free public libraries around the Pittsburgh area. In his lifetime, he spent about $55 million of his own money to build thousands of libraries around the country and around the world. In 1911, Carnegie formed the Carnegie Corporation of New York. The corporation helps educate people and promote peace around the world.

Carnegie again showed great **foresight** when he organized the corporation. He wrote to the board members that they should use the money as they saw fit for the changing times. He recognized that his corporation's good works could last longer than present-day opinions.

This cartoon of Carnegie and his generous gifts to libraries across the United States was published in 1903.

Other Gifts

Carnegie's fortune helped him establish more than 2,500 public libraries around the world. In addition, he gave money to other places where he thought people could better themselves, such as museums and colleges. He formed the Carnegie Institute of Technology in 1900. In 1967, it joined the Mellon Institute to create Carnegie Mellon University, which still operates near Pittsburgh. Many other foundations and trusts in the United States and Europe were funded by Carnegie.

A Legacy

Carnegie was deeply invested in creating world peace. He supported creating an international group that would work toward it. For his efforts toward peace around the world and his generosity, Carnegie was made a commander of the Legion of Honour in France. He was also given the Order of Orange-Nassau, a great honor from the royal family in the Netherlands.

Furthermore, Carnegie did a great deal of writing about his business practices. Many of these writings remain influential to people who study business today. When Carnegie died in 1919, he had given away about $350 million of his fortune. This money is still at work today around the world. Carnegie was successful as an entrepreneur, but he was also successful as a citizen of mankind.

Reports say Carnegie was pleased when he heard of the formation of the League of Nations, an international peacekeeping organization created after World War I.

A Timeline of Andrew Carnegie's Life

1835 — Andrew Carnegie is born in Scotland.

1848 — The Carnegie family comes to the United States.

1853 — Thomas A. Scott hires Carnegie as his secretary.

1859 — Carnegie becomes superintendent of the Pittsburgh division of the Pennsylvania Railroad.

1861 — The Civil War breaks out. Carnegie works as the superintendent of the military railways and the Union's telegraph lines.

1865 — The Keystone Bridge Company is founded. With his brother's help, Carnegie forms Union Iron Mills.

1868 — Carnegie learns of the Bessemer process for creating steel. He adopts it in his factories, making steel a major U.S. industry.

1889 — Carnegie combines his steel holdings to form the Carnegie Steel Company. Carnegie writes "The Gospel of Wealth."

1892 — The Homestead Strike occurs.

1901 — J. P. Morgan buys the Carnegie Steel Company for $480 million, creating U.S. Steel.

1911 — Carnegie founds the Carnegie Corporation of New York to fund his philanthropic work.

1914 — World War I breaks out.

1919 — Carnegie dies in Massachusetts.

Glossary

benefactor: Someone who helps others, often by giving money, time, or expertise.

bobbin: A small, round part around which thread is wound.

degrade: To make lower in rank or status.

depression: A period of economic hardship for an area or country.

dividend: The payment someone receives after investing in a company.

foresight: The ability to see or imagine what will be needed in the future.

immigrant: Someone who moves to a new country to live.

legacy: Someone's lasting influence.

philanthropy: Goodwill to people, often shown by giving money or time for the betterment of mankind.

technology: Tools and scientific knowledge.

telegraph: A tool used for communication that uses wires and electrical signals.

shareholder: Someone who owns a share, or part, in a company.

Index

Websites

Due to the changing nature of Internet links, PowerKids Press has developed an online list of websites related to the subject of this book. This site is updated regularly. Please use this link to access the list: www.powerkidslinks.com/entre/carn